Living the Christian life

'Reading this little book is like taking a short brisk walk on the Haworth moor. It is invigorating and refreshing. A no-nonsense exhortation to Christians, full to the brim of simple wholesome Bible food.'

Mick Lockwood
Minister, Hall Green Chapel, Haworth, West Yorkshire

'Although regarded as one of the great Evangelical leaders of the 18th century, William Grimshaw's writings have been inaccessible to successive generations. Paul and Faith Cook are to be greatly commended for presenting today's readers with a sampling of what made Grimshaw the important leader he was. The brief biographical introduction, coupled with selections from Grimshaw's previously unpublished manuscripts, make a perfect introduction to him. *Living the Christian life* will not only teach you about this important minister historically, but will also benefit you spiritually as you imbibe his practical and experiential emphases.'

Joel R. Beeke, President,
Puritan Reformed Theological Seminary, Grand Rapids, USA

'This collection of recently discovered Grimshaw manuscripts makes an excellent introduction to one of the mightiest, if least known, evangelical preachers of the eighteenth century. William Grimshaw of Haworth was a moralist before he became a Christian; when he did, the change in his heart and life went deep. His preaching became earnest, and his piety became evident. This can be seen in these writings, which form a rich and much needed blend of scriptural doctrine and personal godliness. They serve to introduce us to Grimshaw, but, more importantly, to Grimshaw's God, and show us what it means truly to love God with all our heart.'

Rev. Dr Iain D. Campbell
Free Church of Scotland, Back, Isle of Lewis

Living the Christian life

Selected thoughts
of William Grimshaw
of Haworth

Paul and Faith Cook

PUBLISHING WITH A MISSION

EP BOOKS
Faverdale North, Darlington, DL3 0PH, England

e-mail: sales@evangelicalpress.org

EP BOOKS INC.
P. O. Box 825, Webster, New York 14580, USA

e-mail: usa.sales@evangelicalpress.org

web: http://www.epbooks.org

First published 2008

British Library Cataloguing in Publication Data available

ISBN-13   978-0-85234-691-4   ISBN 0-85234-691-3

Unless otherwise indicated, all Scripture quotations are from the Holy Bible, Authorized (King James) Version.

Printed and bound in Great Britain by MPG Biddles Ltd, King's Lynn, Norfolk

Contents

An explanation...

William Grimshaw of Haworth in Yorkshire, born 14 September 1708, was regarded by J. C. Ryle as one of the three greatest men of the eighteenth-century Evangelical Revival; the other two being John Wesley and George Whitefield. And yet he is little known today.

One reason for this is that he left behind no printed sermons — nothing that posterity could read and profit from after his death — or so it was thought, until the Methodist historian Frank Baker unearthed four manuscripts which Grimshaw had prepared for publication. Baker used these for his doctoral thesis on

Grimshaw, published in 1963, two hundred years after the preacher's death.

Sometimes preaching up to thirty times a week in towns and villages throughout Yorkshire and beyond, William Grimshaw had little time and perhaps available finance to see his work through the press. On his death at the age of fifty-four, his manuscripts were retained in the family and eventually sold to an earlier Methodist historian, Luke Tyerman. Tyerman arranged for them to be stored in the Methodist archives and a full century would pass before these pithy and wise comments would be rediscovered. Then, surprisingly, they appeared to be lost once more. Anxious to obtain them for my forthcoming biography on William Grimshaw in 1996, I made urgent enquiries regarding their whereabouts. Eventually they were discovered among unclassified material at the John Rylands University Library of Manchester, passed there from the Hartley Victoria College.

With full photocopies of all these manuscripts in our possession, each neatly written in Grimshaw's immaculate hand, my husband Paul and I have realized that we have a duty to share some of these treasures of wisdom and pastoral insight with the wider Christian public.

An explanation

As this year is the three-hundredth anniversary of William Grimshaw's birth, it seemed appropriate to mark the occasion in this way.

Three out of the four manuscripts have been used, and the quotations classified in accordance with the various subjects with which Grimshaw was dealing. They remain today as evocative and challenging as when they were first written. A few minor alterations have been made to clarify the text and to remove some obsolete words, but otherwise the wording, apart from the headings, is William Grimshaw's original work.

Perhaps Grimshaw himself should have the last word:

O Christians, give all your glory to him who gave his all for you! All you have received is from God, let all you have be returned to God. The more God's hand is enlarged in blessing you, the more should your hearts be enlarged in blessing God.

Faith Cook
October 2008

William Grimshaw (1708-1763)

William Grimshaw
— evangelist of the North

Early days

That a village like Haworth, situated in the Pennines uplands, should have obtained worldwide renown is quite remarkable. The Brontë sisters and their writings continue to attract widespread interest and pilgrimage. But Haworth itself has long been in danger of forgetting another local character apart from whose influence there would have been no Brontës in the village, and *Wuthering Heights* would never have been written.

To Ted Hughes, the late Poet Laureate, brought up in the locality of nearby Heptonstall, William Grimshaw's influence was still reverberating around his boyhood haunts in the 1930s. 'To judge by the shock-wave which could still be felt, he struck the whole region "like a planet",' he wrote. 'To a degree he changed the very landscape. His heavenly fire, straight out of Blake's *Prophetic Books,* shattered the terrain into biblical landmarks: quarries burst open like craters, and chapels — the bedrock transfigured — materialised standing in them. Gradually it dawned on me', he concluded, 'that I was living among the survivors, in the remains.' The poet was referring to the tremendous impact which William Grimshaw and his preaching had made upon the area, and, we might add, upon the north of England generally.

In his *Journal* John Wesley has the following entry: 'I have been for some days with Mr Grimshaw... A few such as him would make a nation tremble. He carries fire wherever he goes.' So who then was this William Grimshaw and what were his achievements?

We must not omit the fact that Grimshaw was a Lancastrian, born in Brindle, a sleepy little village between Blackburn and Chorley, on 14 September 1708. Neither his father nor mother appeared to have any vital spiritual life at that time. Admitted to Christ's

College, Cambridge, in April 1726 at the early, but not unusual, age of seventeen, he was 'sober and diligent' for the first two years. But in the third year, to quote his own words, 'falling in with bad company, I learned to drink, swear, and become as vile as the worst'. This was no obstacle to ordination, however, either then or now. In 1731 he became curate in charge of Littleborough, near Rochdale, where his heavy drinking and worldly way of life continued. After six months he moved to Todmorden. The inhabitants of the district between Todmorden and Halifax at that time were 'wild, uncouth, and rugged as their native hills'. No traveller could pass that way in safety. The local barbarity gave rise, in Daniel Defoe's opinion, to the proverbial saying:

From Hell, Hull and Halifax,
Good Lord, deliver us.

Grimshaw was little better than the average inhabitant. His main interests were fishing, playing cards, and hunting; and his pastoral visits were usually occasions for heavy drinking and merrymaking. But he was not without pangs of conscience, with the result that he suffered periods of remorse and self-reproach.

Spiritual awakening

He sought to improve the moral standards within his parish; but failing to preach the gospel, he resorted to some bizarre methods. When a young man in the parish made a girl pregnant, but refused to do what was regarded as the honourable thing by marrying her, Grimshaw determined to teach him a lesson. He dressed up as the devil, in dark clothing with horns and a tail — as people imagined him to be. He then concealed himself near a stile over which the youth came each day as he returned from work at dusk. Rising up from the shadows with terrifying appearance, the disguised Grimshaw grasped the young man with an iron grip, and threatened to take him back to Hades with him for his refusal to marry the girl. The youth was scared out of his wits and solemnly promised to put matters right.

One day in 1734 Grimshaw was asked to help a young married couple whose baby had suffered a 'cot death'. He advised them 'to put away all gloomy thoughts, and to get into merry company, and divert themselves, and all would soon be right', which sounds very much like some of our modern psychotherapy! It failed, and again he was sent for; but he had to confess to the parents that he was unable to help them. This experience of his own spiritual inadequacy shook him so much that from that time onwards a new seriousness entered his life. And he began to seek the Lord.

Marriage and reawakening

However, his awakening was mainly moral in character. He began to warn his parishioners of their spiritual danger, and to urge them to live upright lives. 'My friends,' he cried in the middle of a service, 'we are in a damnable state, and I scarcely know how we are to get out of it.' The time of his own release from the bondage of sin had not yet come. But what did arrive — and this diverted him from his spiritual concerns — was a dashing young widow, Sarah Sutcliffe, who had had him in her sights. With breathtaking initiative and audacity, she rode past his lodgings on her horse, calling out to him, 'I am come to bid a penny at you!' Like many another unsuspecting young man in similar circumstances he fell for her, and married this well-to-do heiress soon after. Though he loved her deeply, his wife was of little help to him spiritually.

Yet God had not let him go. In 1738 he experienced another spiritual quickening and gave himself to much prayer and self-examination. He kept a large folio ledger in which he entered his sins on one page and his good works on the opposite page, but he found himself always in spiritual debt to God. He knew he was not right with God, but despite an outward reformation of life and a new seriousness in his pastoral work, he was still in bondage of soul and knew nothing of real peace with God or of forgiveness for his sins.

Justification by faith

In 1739 Grimshaw's wife died, leaving him with two small children, and utterly desolate. He experienced a terrible time of fierce temptation and spiritual conflict, when everything holy was threatened by blasphemous thoughts and fearful doubt. Satan was sifting him; but God was bringing him to the end of himself.

Then, one day early in 1742 he picked up a book in the house of a friend and, instantly, a strange flash of heat seemed to strike him on the face. He opened the book to look at the title page, and discovered it to be by Dr John Owen on *Justification by Faith* and, again, he felt another flash of heat. In whatever way we may attempt to explain this strange phenomenon, Grimshaw himself believed it was a heaven-sent sign. He read of how '...the conscience of a distressed sinner may attain assured peace with God through our Lord Jesus Christ'.

Here, at last, was help for the poor tormented soul of William Grimshaw. Having read the book through, he exclaimed, 'O what light and comfort did I now enjoy in my own soul, and what a taste of the pardoning love of God!' His seven years of seeking and searching were at an end.

Revival at Haworth

The joys of salvation were reflected immediately in Grimshaw's preaching. His emphasis now fell upon salvation by faith alone, through the imputation of Christ's righteousness, and no longer upon the works of man's righteousness. Some accused him of preaching a novel doctrine, but he demonstrated from the *Thirty-Nine Articles* that this was not so. A degree of success followed his preaching at Todmorden but, having married again, he moved to Haworth where he became 'perpetual curate in charge'. Sadly, his second wife died after five years. Later he would cast lots to determine whether or not to remarry, but a toss of the gold Joannes coin from Portugal indicated the negative, and so he remained single for the rest of his life.

Grimshaw had no sooner settled in Haworth in 1742 when the beginnings of a remarkable revival of religion appeared. The events which followed, and indeed throughout the twenty-one years of his ministry there, soon made him the acknowledged leader of the Evangelical Revival in the north of England.

Benjamin Ingham, a former member of the group of Oxford students known as the 'Holy Club', and John Nelson, converted under John Wesley in London, were instrumental in establishing many religious societies in the West Riding of Yorkshire during the early years of the revival, but in 1742 Grimshaw was only vaguely aware of what was going on elsewhere. The revival in Haworth, in fact, was a local manifestation of a far greater work of God which had been taking place in the London and Bristol areas and in parts of the West Riding. The repercussions of the Haworth revival were eventually to extend into all the adjoining counties.

When Grimshaw went to Haworth it was one of the most important centres for the worsted clothing industry, with much of the work being done in the local homes. The people were tough, of an independent character, and with few human graces. The rugged, straight-speaking, no-nonsense Grimshaw appealed to them. His dedication and burning zeal for their eternal interests soon deeply affected them. The handful of worshippers on his arrival quickly expanded into overflowing congregations.

The church building held about a thousand hearers, but soon many could only find room in the churchyard. People flocked from other parishes to listen to the preacher who told them how their sins could be forgiven.

Haworth Church in 1756

When George Whitefield and both John and Charles Wesley later preached there, the extensive graveyard would be thronged with people, numbering upwards of six thousand. Under the preaching many were seized with strong conviction of sin and cried aloud for mercy. Grimshaw sought, through the power of Jesus Christ, to turn people from a love of sin to a love of righteousness. He believed strongly in the duty of rebuking sin. On one occasion he was in a local shop, when a man came in who was well known for his serial adulteries. Grimshaw immediately announced to all in the shop, 'The devil has been very busy in this neighbourhood. I can touch the man with my stick who lay with another man's wife last night: the end of these things will be death, the ruin of body and soul for ever.'

In the summer of 1743 Grimshaw began to organize his converts into small groups, and he visited and exhorted them in their cottage meetings throughout his parish and surrounding areas. At first he was reluctant to cross parish boundaries, but the spiritual needs of people who were largely neglected by other clergymen persuaded him to do it.

The daily lives of the people were soon affected by the revival. Immorality and foul language declined. Homes ruined by alcohol and physical abuse were restored.

We read that 'Families in which sin had made the most miserable havoc, and in which all the comforts of life were destroyed, now were made happy in the fear of God.'

The horsewhip story

Mrs Gaskell, the novelist, is responsible for the story that Grimshaw used to horsewhip drinkers from the local pubs into church. She wrote ninety years after Grimshaw's death and the story arose from her vivid imagination. But like most embroidered stories there was some basis of fact. Grimshaw did check the churchyard, the nearby streets and alehouses for 'idlers' during the psalm sung before the sermon. Those he found were firmly directed into the church with that authority common to the 'parson' of those days.

Two colourful incidents were the likely material for Mrs Gaskell's story. On one occasion Grimshaw sent out two churchwardens to check up on any parishioners idling their time away in the public houses, instead of attending worship. The psalm had finished, but the churchwardens had not reappeared. So Grimshaw himself went out in search of the wardens whilst the congregation waited. After a while, heavy footsteps were heard approaching. The porch door flew open, and the stentorian tones of Grimshaw's voice were heard: 'What think you! What think you!' he boomed. 'The churchwardens who went out to detect others and prevent them from sinning, I have found in the inn drinking a pint of ale! For shame! For shame!' he cried, as he remounted the steps to his pulpit, and the churchwardens sneaked shamefacedly back into their seats.

The other incident did most to give rise to Mrs Gaskell's story of the horsewhip. A group of unruly youths had been taking delight in jostling and assaulting some of Grimshaw's congregation in a nearby village as they gathered to attend a weekly prayer-meeting. So after this had happened two or three times, the leader of the meeting reported the incidents to Grimshaw who asked to be kept informed.

Once again the same hooligans set upon the people as they gathered; but this time Grimshaw, disguised in a greatcoat, had joined the youths as though he were one of them. The night was dark, and they failed to recognize the burly figure of the curate, as he urged them onwards, from the back of the group. Gradually he inched the gang down a passageway to the lighted doorway of the cottage where the meeting was to be held. Then, with one mighty heave, he pushed the youths into the room and slammed the door. Still blinking in the light, they scarcely realized what was happening when their new companion suddenly produced a horsewhip from under his coat and 'dealt round its utmost virtue on the astonished clowns until his vigorous arm was tired'. Having suitably chastised them, Grimshaw then fell on his knees and pleaded with great earnestness for their souls.

'As a beast to market'

Many amazing conversions took place during the revival. One woman recounted how she and her husband, former Quakers living six miles from Haworth, were brought to salvation. Her husband went to Haworth out of curiosity and was converted. He then tried to persuade his wife to go with him to hear Grimshaw. 'I'll not go to hear that black devil,' she retorted. Constant pleas failed to move her, so one day he forcibly dressed her in her Sunday best, took a rod and drove her the six miles to Haworth. 'He drove me', she said, 'as men drive a beast to market; I went calling and abusing Mr Grimshaw all the way.'

However, the preaching brought her under conviction, and the following Sunday she returned to Haworth of her own accord. Grimshaw noticed her distress, sought her out after the service, and told her that on a certain day he would come and preach in their home. That farmhouse became one of his regular preaching centres and she was one of the first of the 'great number' converted there under his preaching.

Grimshaw's preaching

Grimshaw preached to congregations in Haworth numbering between a thousand and twelve hundred. He spoke plainly in what he called 'market language'. Many of the people were uneducated and illiterate, so he used common speech coloured with the imagery of daily life. 'If you perish,' he would warn, 'you will perish with the sound of the gospel in your lugs!' Urging the young people to repent, he exclaimed, 'Do not think you can dance with the devil all day and then feast with Christ at night.'

Pressing home the duty of all men to thank God for the blessings of food and drink, he pointedly commented: 'Some of you are worse than the very swine; for the pigs will gruff over their victuals, but you say nothing.'

He could hold a congregation spellbound for two hours or more, with many moved to tears as the Word of God came to them with convicting power. When preaching in the open air on the Prodigal Son, one listener recalled him calling out with great energy: 'Yonder he comes! Yonder he comes, all in rags; yonder he comes, rag, tag and bobtail!' And the crowd turned to look in the direction he was pointing, to catch a glimpse of the returning prodigal.

A Puritan on the warpath

One writer has described Grimshaw as 'a Puritan on the warpath'. Like all true preachers sent by God he had a zeal for righteousness. Many colourful anecdotes have been told of his determination to deal with sin in its various blatant expressions. The annual horse races and wakes held on the moors above Haworth was an event of much worldliness. Grimshaw made representations to the organizers but without success, so he announced that he would resort to man no more and instead would seek the ear of his God. This he did. Race week arrived with the usual large crowds intent on an orgy of riot and drunkenness. But the heavens opened, and for three days torrential rain fell, leading to a cancellation of the races, never again to be resumed.

The young people were in the habit of indulging in a variety of sports and less desirable occupations on Sunday afternoons on the moors above Haworth. On weekdays Grimshaw often enjoyed a game with them himself, but preached against using the Lord's Day for such activities. His words availed little, so finally Grimshaw took to strolling across the moors himself to rebuke those concerned. Vaulting five-bar gates was no problem for the new curate, as the young people soon discovered, for though they kept a sharp look-out for the approach of 'the parson', they were regularly spotted and reproved.

Sometimes Grimshaw would use disguise to detect the true nature of things among his parishioners. One of several accounts concerns a man and his wife whose professions to holiness of life Grimshaw suspected. He had heard that they were tight-fisted and unmerciful towards the needy. So, borrowing a weaver's shabby jacket and cap, he dressed up as a poor beggar in urgent need of food and a night's lodging. The man of the house was unmoved by his entreaties, at which point Grimshaw removed his disguise and delivered a lecture on covetousness and hard-heartedness.

Evangelizing the North

As a result of Grimshaw's preaching, there came into being in that area of Yorkshire what was called the Haworth Round, a string of preaching centres sustained by the indefatigable labours of William Grimshaw, ably helped by other men whose hearts God had touched.

In 1747 Grimshaw had a deep spiritual experience which altered the course of his ministry.

He wrote:

> ...my mind was deeply affected with strong impressions to preach the gospel abroad [in more distant places]; the event [result] I left to the Lord, fearing to be disobedient to what I trust was the heavenly call.

He obeyed without delay, and set off on a preaching tour which was to be typical of many such excursions throughout the following years: Todmorden, Rossendale, Bacup, Rochdale and Manchester ... as well as the many farms and hamlets too insignificant to be named on a map.

He preached three or four times each day and was always back in Haworth for the Sunday services.

He identified himself with the Methodists and with leaders such as Ingham, Nelson, Charles and John Wesley, William Darney and George Whitefield. The 'Methodists' at that time consisted of men and women whose hearts God had touched and brought to a living faith in Christ. They continued for fifty years within the Church of England, but met together in their 'societies' for spiritual edification.

Plaque on wall at Sowden's, Grimshaw's home

Despite opposition from the clergy and hostile mobs, nothing now could hold William Grimshaw back.

If I find the Lord's pleasure be that I must launch out further, I will obey; for he daily convinces me more and more what he has graciously done and will do for my soul. O I can never do enough in gratitude and love to him, for the least mite, if I may reverently so speak, of what his blessings are to me.

So for the next sixteen years of his life he devoted his physical and mental powers to spreading the gospel in many different parts of the north of England. He rarely preached less than twenty times a week and on occasions preached as many as thirty times. Occasionally he experienced severe persecution, such as when his life was endangered at Roughlee in August 1748.

The pulpit of Haworth church in those days was a three-decker with two texts inscribed upon it. One of these was I Corinthians 2:2: 'For I determined not to know anything among you, save Jesus Christ, and him crucified.' That was central in all Grimshaw's preaching wherever he went. The glorious gospel of Jesus Christ radiated out from the unlikely centre of Haworth to Keighley, Bingley, Bradford, Halifax, Leeds and most of the other towns and villages of the West Riding; and beyond to Otley, York, Pocklington, Hull, Sheffield, Glossop, Stockport, Manchester, Blackburn, Preston, Clitheroe, Kendal and numerous other villages and towns in the north of England.

He travelled on horseback and on foot, preaching in parish churches, but more often in barns and cottages and in the open air, urging men and women to repent and seek the mercy of God in Jesus Christ. Towards the close of his life he declared:

At home and abroad my work is the same: 'tis to preach Jesus, and him crucified; and to help, through him, poor sinners to God, grace and glory.

He had great compassion for the people. One day he was preaching near Colne, and holding out Christ to sinners regardless of how far they had wandered from God or deeply sinned. Then, spotting a white-haired old man in the front row, Grimshaw said kindly: 'And for thee too, old moss-crop.' This was the term of endearment he used back in Haworth to describe elderly members of his congregation.

Conclusion

Much more could be said in connection with William Grimshaw. Some aspects of his life and ministry have been omitted entirely. Reference has been made to one of two Scripture texts he had inscribed on his pulpit. The other one was 'For to me to live is Christ, and to die is gain.' Those words of the apostle Paul sum up Grimshaw's life. In one of his letters he wrote:

Christ is my meat; Christ is my drink;
My Christ on whom I call;
Christ is my Prophet, Priest and King;
My Christ is all in all.

Zeal and love for Christ motivated him in all he did. Someone who had lived in his house and had opportunity of observing his life wrote, 'He would often say, "I love my Saviour, but how shall I love him enough?" He was so filled with love that at only the mentioning of the name of God he has stood still, ten minutes together.'

If to live was Christ, then to die was gain for Grimshaw. He had no fear of death. When a typhus epidemic broke out in Haworth early in 1763, he sensed that the Lord would call him. He caught the fever, and gave instructions that the sermon to be preached at his funeral was to be on Philippians 1:21 — 'For to me to live is Christ and to die is gain,' — and that these words should be on the lid of his coffin.

When Benjamin Ingham visited him a few days before he died, Grimshaw greeted him with the words, 'My last enemy is come! The signs of death are on me, but I am not afraid. No! No! Blessed be God, my hope is sure, and I am in his hands.' And near the end he said, 'I am quite exhausted, but I shall soon be home, for ever with the Lord — a poor miserable sinner redeemed by his blood.' And so he died on 7 April 1763, aged fifty-four — one of the greatest men this country has known. His Herculean labours, energized by love for God and motivated by compassion for his fellow men, did more to establish vital Christian faith in the north of England than the endeavours of any other man. The Christian church should remember him with thanksgiving to God.

The following sections drawn from three of his unpublished treatises will give the reader a good impression of the man and of his convictions regarding the character of the Christian life.

Paul Cook

The character of a Christian

In a short unpublished manuscript
William Grimshaw gives six descriptions
of the true Christian,
entitling his work

The nature, state and conduct
of a Christian.

The nature, state and conduct of a Christian

A penitent man

The true Christian is a penitent though a pardoned man. The length of his repentance is as long as his life. He daily repents, because he daily offends. But his repentance is not so much out of fear as for unkindness. The wrong of his sins trouble him more than the danger... When he finds his soul loaded with guilt he gives it over to his spiritual physician, Jesus, from whom he receives cordials and cures answerable to his complaints.

A humble man

The true Christian is a humble man. He is a friendly enemy to himself, for though he is not out of favour with himself, no man esteems him less than himself, not out of ignorance or negligence but out of a voluntary meek dejectedness. His eyes are full of other men's perfections and of his own wants [deficiencies]. He would rather honour than be honoured. His manner is one of lowliness without affectation, and he really is what he seems.

A patient man

The true Christian is a patient man. He is made of mettle not so hard as flexible. His shoulders are broad — fit for a load of injuries which he bears, not cowardly because he dares not avenge, but courageously because he may not. He has so conquered himself that wrongs cannot conquer him, and finds that victory consists in yielding … His hopes are so strong that they can surmount all discouragement.

An honest man

The true Christian is an honest man. He looks not at what he might do, but what he should. He is simply and sincerely upright … He has but one heart, and that lies open to sight. He uses no reserves but what discretion honestly requires. His word is his bond and his 'Yea' his oath which he will not violate for fear or loss. With him it is not 'This I saw not' but 'This I said'. All his dealings are square and above board. He tells the faults of what he sells and restores the unforeseen gain of a mistake made in reckoning.

A faithful man

The true Christian is a faithful man. He walks every day with his Maker and talks familiarly with him. He lives always in heaven and all earthly things seem under his feet. When he goes in to converse with God he wears not his own clothes, but always takes them out of the Redeemer's wardrobe. The things of this world he deals with as a stranger and has his heart ever at Home. His war is perpetual and without a truce — his victory is certain and his crown is glorious. If his hand is wounded, his heart is safe, and though he is sometimes foiled yet is he never vanquished.

A happy man

The true Christian is a happy man. He reads himself more than all books and so perfectly learns his lesson as never to forget it. He knows the world, but cares not for it. He has gained such an ascendancy over his heart as to cross his will without a mutiny. In natural things he wishes no more than nature needs and in spiritual things is ever graciously ambitious … Upon him all smaller crosses fall as hailstones upon a roof, and as for greater calamities he can accept them as tokens of love … He can make his cottage a palace or his croft a kingdom when he wishes because he has learnt that a man's greatness or baseness is within himself.

He walks cheerfully in the way that God has chalked out for him and never wishes it to be wider or smoother than God has made it. He is strengthened by the temptations that foil him. He comes forth crowned and triumphing out of every spiritual battle and every scar he receives makes him beautiful. His eyes are so fastened on heaven that no earthly object can remove them. Yea, his whole self is there before his time.

The Christian esteems it no great matter to live and his greatest business is to die. He has become so intimate with death that he neither apprehends nor fears any unkindness from him. He makes no more of dying than when he is weary of falling asleep. Whether he lives, he lives unto the Lord. For whether living or dying he is the Lord's. For him to live is Christ and to die is gain, and he is well provided for both worlds.

The life of a Christian

The Believer's Golden Chain
was the title that William Grimshaw gave to another
of his unpublished manuscripts. In the introductory
paragraph he writes:

You are here presented with a golden chain of twenty links. Wear it, in the words of the Wiseman, as 'an ornament of grace on thy head and a chain about thy neck'.

The believer's golden chain

The believer's aims

To be consistent

Set the watch of your lives by the Sun of Righteousness. Live in print and keep the copy of your lives free from blots and blurs that all may read the example clearly. Live so that the Word which has brought salvation to your souls may bring your souls to salvation; we must first shine in grace before we can shine in glory.

To be content

Be willing to go without whatever God is not willing to give. We receive immensely more good than we deserve. We should not murmur therefore though we enjoy little good, nor complain when we suffer much evil. If God is not pleased to give us riches, let us be willing to lack riches. If God is not willing to give us health, let us be willing to lack health. If God is not willing to give us children, let us be willing to lack children. Therefore submit your will to God's will. He who submits his will to God shall obtain his will from God. Has he not said, 'I will never, never leave you; I will never, never, never forsake you'? (cf. Hebrews 13:5). He who said it will not unsay it. Therefore take up your contentment in God's appointment.

To be thankful

They can never praise God enough who have tasted the goodness of God. Should they not bless God the most who are the most blessed? Those who hold the largest farms must pay the largest rents. The greater the mercies, the greater must be the duties … No good lives so long as that which is thankfully improved. No evil dies so soon as that which is patiently endured. To bless God for mercies is a way to increase them. To bless God for miseries is the way to remove them. All you have is received from God; let all you have be returned to God. Has he made you sons while others remain slaves? Has he made you heirs of glory while others remain heirs of wrath? This he has done, and more, for you, believer. What unspeakable, inconceivable cause have you in heart, lip and life to bless his holy name! Surely, surely, where the sun of mercy shines the hottest, the fruits of grace should grow the fairest.

To learn humility from Christ's humility

The most lowly believer is the most lovely believer. They are most like Christ who says, 'Learn of me, for I am meek and lowly in heart, and you shall find rest unto your souls' (Matthew 11:29). The most holy are always the most humble. It is good to have abasing thoughts of ourselves. The clothes of humility should always be worn on the back of Christianity. The Lord has his city house and his country house. The heaven of heavens is his city house and the hearts of the humble his country house... Keep your souls out of pride and pride out of your souls or pride will keep God out of your souls and your souls out of heaven. Alas, to be proud of our gifts, graces and spiritual blessings is not only dangerous but damnable. What is there that you have not received? A humble heart knows no fountain but God's grace and an upright man knows no end but God's glory.

The believer's endeavours

To do as much good as you can

Do good in the world with the goods of the world. The goods we get will leave us; the good we do will never leave us. He who will show no mercy will have no mercy shown him. Let compassion be your shop to trade in and heaven shall be your house to dwell in.

He who relieves the poor saints for Christ's sake shall be rewarded by Christ for the saints' sake ... That is not cast away that is cast into Christ's treasury. Though it makes your purse lighter, it will make your crown heavier.

To improve the time you have

Time ere long will be to you time no longer (Revelation 10:6). Opportunities are for eternity, but not to eternity. No time is ours but the present, and that in a moment is past. Consider also how much of your time is gone, and yet how little of your work is done. Your time is short and your work is great. You have a Christ to believe in, a God to honour, a soul to save, a race to run, a crown to win, a hell to escape and a heaven to gain. You have many strong corruptions to subdue, many weak graces to confirm, many temptations to resist and many afflictions to bear, many mercies to improve and many duties to perform. Therefore endeavour to improve your time. All the time that God allows us is little enough to perform the task he allots us … Today is better than tomorrow. Today is your living day; tomorrow is your dying day. Now if ever, now or never, up and be doing, lest you be for ever undone.

To use the means of grace diligently

Be diligent in using the means of grace, but do not make an idol of them. Prayer, praise, reading, meditation, self-examination must be daily diligently and seriously observed. We must be daily in private and family prayer, and regular in public worship. Let prayer be your daily work and your first and last work daily. Christians can never lack time for prayer if they have a heart for prayer.

But do not make an idol of the means of grace. What is *hearing* without Christ, but like a cabinet without a jewel; or receiving the Lord's Supper without Christ, but like an empty glass without a cordial? Means of grace can never have too much of our diligence, but 'When we have done all, we are unprofitable servants' (cf. Luke 17:10). But look in them and through them at Christ and in him and through him for grace and holiness, heaven and happiness. Then all will be well.

To give and accept reproof

Take those reproofs best which you need the most. Do not be angry at those who tell you the truth, nor with the truth that is told you. He can be no true friend to you who is a friend to your sins; and you can be no friend to yourself if you are offended at him who tells you of your

interestingly stated

sins. Would you love him the worse who would have you the better?

And let me here observe that as in *receiving* reproofs we should do it patiently and thankfully, so in *giving* reproofs we should do it wisely and faithfully, even though our reproofs are repaid with reproaches or worse. Reproof should not be with passion but with compassion, not with laughter but with weeping. It is the part of a good man to reprove, though his reproofs are not taken in good part. Is it better to love the smiles of men and to lose their souls?

How to grow in grace

Give God your heart

'My son, give me thy heart' (Proverbs 23:26). Yes, our God demands the heart. The heart is the field out of which God looks for a plentiful crop of glory. If the heart be for God, all is for God. Our affections, wills, desires, tears, time, strength, prayer, giving, estates, bodies, souls, all, all are for God. The obedience of the heart is the heart of obedience. The heart is the presence chamber of the King of Glory. That which is most worthy in us should be entirely his, who is most worthy. The body is but the cabinet, the soul is the jewel. There are too many professing Christians, it may be feared, who have no mind to give God their hearts. O my dear souls! Let hearts and lips, let words and works, let prayers and practice go together. A little done with the heart is far better than a great deal done without the heart … He who regards the heart will only regard that which is done with the heart. 'Son, give me thy heart.'

Crucify your sins

Crucify your sins that have crucified Christ. Were the rocks rent when Christ died for our sins? And shall not our hearts be rent that have lived in our sins? The nails that pierced his hands should now pierce our hearts. That should now grieve our spirits that grieved his spirit. O! put sin to death which put Christ to death. We may blame Judas for his treachery and the Jews for their cruelty, but the truth is, it was ourselves and our iniquity that crucified the Lord of life and glory... Let the cry of your prayers outcry the cries of your sins.

Strive more for inward purity than outward happiness

Gold in your bags may make you greater but it is grace in your hearts that will make you better. A heavenly conversation is immensely preferable to all earthly possessions. It is a great mercy to have a portion in the world; but to have the world for your portion is a great misery. What an excellent thing is godliness! Who would not part with all for it? Who would not count all other things but dross in comparison? But alas, the world is diligent about temporal things, but negligent of eternal things, careful about dying vanities, but careless about immortal excellencies, feasting their bodies but starving their soul.

O! what is darkness to light? What is gold to grace? What is earth to heaven that many so shamelessly neglect the great and weighty and vital things and busy themselves about straws and feathers. I beseech you, labour more for inward holiness than outward happiness; more for the seed of grace than the bag of gold, more for inward piety than outward plenty, more for a heavenly conversation than an earthly possession. In a word, while you live you will find godliness gainful, and when you die you will find it needful.

Meditate on death and heaven

Think on death. Death is certain. 'It is appointed unto men once to die,' (Hebrews 9:27). To think about death is death to some men: but let us meditate on death. Meditation on death will put sin to death. He who dies daily is more sure to die happily … When you put off your clothes at night think of putting off your earthly tabernacle. Go to your beds as you would to your grave and close your eyes in this world as you would open them in another. Today is your living day: tomorrow may be your dying day. Meditation on death will prepare you for death.

Think on heaven. Heaven is a place where all joy is enjoyed, mirth without sadness, light without darkness, sweetness without bitterness, rest without labour, plenty without poverty, life without death. O what joy enters into a believer when he enters into the joy of his Saviour! Who would not work for glory with the greatest diligence and wait for glory with the greatest patience? O what glories there are in glory — to be in Christ is heaven below, to be with Christ is heaven above. Let our condition here be never so grand, it is hell without him: or never so poor and miserable, it is heaven with him.

The believer's watchfulness

Let your conduct match your professions

Christians should be burning as well as shining lamps. Should we walk in darkness whose Father is Light? Either let your works match your profession or your profession your works. Never put on Christ's livery to do Satan's drudgery. Alas, my brethren, what avails our profession if we do not live up to it? The almost Christian will never be saved. Therefore I beseech you, be *altogether* Christian: upright, sincere and truly godly. It is good to know and profess, but extremely better to practice. O Christians, not only make a good profession, but be sure to make your profession good.

Search your own heart

No one begins to be good until he knows he is bad. Nor can he relish the sweetness of God's mercies who has never tasted the bitterness of his own miseries. A man may be acquainted with the grace of truth who never knew the truth of grace … Be diligent, I beseech you, in searching your hearts. A man may profess, may pray, may speak, may look, may walk as a Christian and yet be a complete hypocrite.

Consider, Christian, these three things: what you were by nature, what you are in grace and what you shall be in glory. If you are in a state of inward faith, light and life, then you are in Christ and in a state of grace; and if you are in a state of grace then you shall be in a state of glory.

Test all things

Take nothing upon trust; but all upon trial. All is not gold that glisters. All is not truth that goes for truth. Many, like infants, swallow down all. They take in doctrines without trial by the touchstone of God's Word. O, say they, our teacher is an honest, able, learned man; what he tells us is all true. The cup may be of gold, and yet what is in it be poison. God may reject some teachers as copper whom men regard as silver. Why are there so many wretched professors of faith? Because there are so many wretched teachers. Though they talk like angels, regard them not if they walk like devils … Therefore by your teachers' sayings, try their doctrines; by their ways, try their lives; try their worship by the Word of God. We beseech you for the Lord's sake and for your precious souls' sake, take nothing upon trust, but all upon trial.

Preachers to hear, books to read and company to keep

Hear the best men. Hear a soul-searching, a soul-winning, a soul-enriching minister; one who declares the whole counsel of God ... one who makes hard things easy and dark things plain. Many, to gain vain admiration of the ignorant and the praises of men, affect in their preaching high-flying words, pompous language, rhetorical strains and philosophical terms. A sanctified heart in a minister is better than a silver tongue. A heart full of grace is better than a head full of notions ... that which tickles delicate ears does little to relieve diseased spirits.

Read the best books and especially the Bible, that infinitely best of books. Whatever human books you read let them be the most spiritual, precious, pious, holy, soul-sanctifying and heart-searching books, full of precious Christ, our Prophet, Priest and King, comparing what you read with what is written in the Book of God and carefully trying your heart and ways by both.

Forsake all bad company and follow the good. Be much with them who are much with God. Walk with them who walk with God. Let the birds teach you: 'Those of a feather will flock together.' But O! let the apostle John teach you: 'Truly our fellowship is with the Father and with his Son Jesus Christ' (1 John 1:3). Let them be the choicest companions to you who have Christ as the choicest companion to them. Associate with those on earth with whom you hope to associate in heaven.

Christian imperatives

First things first

We must value the best things most highly of all:

a. Knowledge is good, but practice is better — a good understanding without a good life will never turn to a good account.
b. Works are good but faith is better. Faith is a grace that is most needful. True faith is always a working faith, and a working faith is a saving faith.
c. Gifts are good, but grace is better. A sanctified heart is better than a silver tongue.

d. Honour is good, but a pure conscience is better. No amount of flattery can heal a bad conscience.
e. Care of the body is good but care of the soul is better. A Christian's work below is done best when his work for heaven is done first.
f. A peaceable spirit is good, but zeal for truth is better. Love the truth of God, justify his truth and the truth will justify you.
g. Christ is better than all — he is sweeter than wine, better than life. He who came from above is above all. He is life eternal.

Seek to please others, but seek to please God above all. If there is no fellowship between Christ and you in holiness, there will be no fellowship between Christ and you in happiness.

Do not fear suffering

If a righteous cause bring us to suffer, a righteous God will stand by and deliver us. The fear of persecution is more than persecution. Are we members of Christ and afraid to be martyrs for Christ? Though they kill the body, it [persecution] crowns the soul. It only takes from you a life which you cannot keep, and brings you a life which you cannot lose. He who loses a base life for Christ shall find a better life in Christ. Do wicked men glory in that which is their shame, and shall we be ashamed of that which is our glory? It is an honour to be dishonoured for Christ.

Love your fellow believers

Our love must be sincere and not selfish. O dear brethren, let me entreat you to live in love and to live in truth. You are all fellow labourers, fellow members, fellow citizens, fellow travellers, fellow sufferers, fellow servants, and should we not love one another? Consider also, we all have the same Father, God; the same Saviour and Head, Christ; the same life and guide, the Holy Spirit; the same attendants, angels; the same grace, faith; the same title, son; the same clothing, Christ's righteousness; the same glory, heaven; and should we not be dear to one another?

Therefore, dear Christians, let me beseech you to love one another. If you ask how we must show this love, I answer:

Firstly, you should highly esteem each other remembering that God calls his people his jewels, his treasure, his portion, his glory.

Secondly, you should delight in one another's company. God delights in the company of his saints and so should we.

Thirdly, be ready to help one another. 'To do good and to communicate, forget not' (Hebrews 13:16).

And fourthly, sympathize with one another. Fellow members should be fellow-feelers. He who is Love itself commands it.

Keep on to the end

Set out for God at your beginning and hold out with God to your ending. As there are none too old for eternity, there are none too young for mortality. Is it not sad that we should live so long in the world and do so little good? Do not think to dance with the devil all day and sup with Christ at night ... The flower of life is of Christ's setting, and shall it be of the devil's plucking? Will you hang the most sparkling jewel of your young years in the devil's ears? If God's day is too soon for your repentance, your tomorrow will be too late for your acceptance. You can never come too soon to God, nor stay too long with God. O! hold on and hold out to the end. Only he who departs in the faith shall be saved.

The experiences of a Christian

A further manuscript of William Grimshaw's left at his death takes the form of a collection of comments on the spiritual life which he gathered throughout his ministry both from his own personal experience and his pastoral dealings with his congregation. He called it,

Experiences gathered from conversation with my own and the souls of others.

The following are selected from that manuscript.

Experiences gathered from conversation with my own and the souls of others

At the beginning

Different experiences of conversion

There is but one way in nature into this world, and a 100 ways out of it into another; but there are a 100 ways into the spiritual world, or into CHRIST, and but one way, which is CHRIST, into the world to come. Nay, there are not two in 500 of God's children that are born again or brought into CHRIST, every way alike. Therefore, when two or more of them are speaking together concerning the manner in which they were brought to know the Lord, they may well find that they differ from one another in some or even in all respects. Although those present have all clearly experienced the peace of God in their hearts, yet they may depart from each other greatly dissatisfied and be afraid that their experiences are wrong, and those of others are right. Here the devil has a fair opportunity given him of distracting and grieving their minds, when there is no cause or reality for it at all. I must desire my brethren to take notice of this observation. Young inexperienced children are most in danger in this matter.

Early spiritual joys

Great joy is generally a token of true, but not of strong faith. This is the case of the newborn babes in Christ. The change wrought in the instant of new birth or at the manifestation of pardon of sin is so real and exquisite as it is a felt change from soul pain to fervour, to peace and pleasure; from a hell to heaven, that it is rather rapture and ecstasy for a time.

Great joy, or our first love, is but short lived. With some it lasts but a month or two and seldom longer; with others, not more than a week or two; and with many not above a day or two, and sometimes not so long.

This great joy, though God, arising from an exquisite sense of pardon and peace, and an influx of God or heaven into the soul, a bridal bliss in Christ (Matthew 9:15; Luke 17:21; Romans 14:17) is nevertheless encompassed with much flesh [i.e. sinful tendencies]. Such are ready to think all storms are over, and one can scarcely persuade them that they shall be tempted or know sorrow any more. Such, while they are thus full of zeal and prayer and praise, are very apt to censure those as not being Christians, who, though old and deep in grace and spiritual experience, are not so lively (or rather zealous) as themselves.

Temptations for new believers

New believers are by and by, like their Master, led into the wilderness, and that too not merely by permission, but by the Holy Spirit of God.

At this time we think (I mean at our first coming into this wilderness) that we are not God's child, that we are not justified nor pardoned, that we are mistaken with ourselves, that it was only a delusion to think so; now we are grieved that we affirmed our being forgiven to anyone and are ready to recant it. But this is only Satan's suggestion and it is generally the first thing he tempts us with. So it was the first thing with which he tempted our blessed Saviour, to question whether he was the Son of God. If the devil can but make us doubt of this, so long as it prevails, the progress of grace may seem to be totally stopped. Yet all the while this suggestion harries us, we need not be discouraged for a perfect peace void of all condemnation is still experienced in us. And therefore we may boldly charge this temptation upon the devil, and tell him, he's a liar and the father of it.

It is the way of believers, whilst they are young, to look much at their temptations, and but little of their evidence of peace; and by doing so they cause themselves a great deal of needless vexation of heart. And this I take to be a certain sign that they are at most but little children in Christ. But older believers, even in the strongest and longest temptations, always eye their peace and by that means, in the roughest trials are always composed, steady and happy.

We are often the most violently tempted especially on the morning before we receive the Lord's Supper. This is a device of Satan to scare us from the Lord's Table, and to deprive us of the blessing. Therefore the more we are tempted at those seasons, the more resolute we should always be to attend the Lord's Supper. Such temptations are a signal for good.

How to deal with temptations

If a temptation appears to our conception but small and at a great distance, instantly pray, and we may never see more of it for a time; but if we forget or neglect to pray, it will advance and grow larger, our eye and affection will be more and more enamoured with it, until at last we shall find no will to resist it, and so be prevailed upon criminally to consent to it.

When you first see a temptation immediately look up to God in a word of prayer, and you shall immediately be delivered. Sometimes it will return again and again, perhaps a dozen times within the space of five minutes, but will be as often repelled by repeatedly renewing your prayer. There are often very fiery conflicts, especially when the temptations are either lustful or blasphemous ones; but continue instant in prayer, and in a few minutes they will totally cease.

The older we grow in Christ, the less frequent, but the stronger are the temptations that assail us, and the most dangerous temptation is to be seldom tempted. Then we are more likely to be off our guard, and if the devil surprises us with a temptation, we are betrayed into a compliance with it unawares. This plainly shows that a Christian should be always under arms, and never off his watch. Stand, and when you have done all, stand.

Beating Satan with his own weapons

In temptations I find it too little to resist the tempter; resistance is good, but resistance is no victory. I find I must overcome. How is this? I find I must not rest and think myself safe until I've wrested the tempter's sword out of his hand and plunged it into his own heart. When do I find I do this? When I, by the kind of temptation, am driven to the opposite virtue; as when by temptation to lust I apply myself to means and exercises of chastity, by pride to humility, etc. Thus the devil is beat with his own weapons and at last is afraid to tempt me by any means lest I should profit thereby to my soul; become more chaste, more humble, more watchful, more holy etc. Glory be to God for this experience.

If I would do as God would have me do, I find I must then do as the devil does: be always on my watch. I experience incessant occasion for this. Satan is always like a roaring lion, walking about, and seeking whom he may devour. You must watch and pray, says our Lord; you must be sober and vigilant, and resist Satan, steadfast in the faith, says Peter (1 Peter 5:8).

In all sorts of temptations you commit no sin by them as long as your hand or heart, will or desire do not consent nor comply therewith: so long as you feel an enmity, detestation and hatred against them or, let me add, not the least desire after them, you are innocent.

Progressing in the Christian life

Growing in grace

Young believers have their first trials with their *outward* sins and out of love to Jesus are so intent to get rid of them that they seldom think or look at anything more, imagining that if they can but get over them, all strife is over, and all storms are past; but by the time they have, or have nearly, got rid of them, those *inward* sins or corruptions begin to appear. At first sight of them they are apt to think themselves more wicked than ever, and sorely grieve over their condition. But by and by or if they are persevering Christians, they resolutely toil on and indefatigably labour to purge them all away through the Word, prayer and fasting.

In the progress of grace, we should always take care to keep what we have, and strive continually for more; and the present grace is always the best kept when it is the most exercised, as well as being the surest means to procure greater measures. To him that has shall be given and he shall have abundance.

A Christian must never look back or stand still in grace, thinking that he has already sufficiently attained. Forgetting what is behind he must press forward to that which is before. If he looks back, it must be chiefly for these two ends: to praise God for what he has received, and to encourage him to look earnestly and continually by prayer to God for more. For these ends he can never look back too much.

Two sorts of sins and two sorts of temptations

In our regenerate state two corruptions chiefly plague us and cost us more pains than all besides to subdue them.

The one is our *constitutional* sin, which we were most addicted to in nature. This is what the apostle Paul calls 'the sin which doth so easily beset us' (Hebrews 12:1). The other is lust. Consequently, he whose constitutional infirmity is the latter has but one to struggle with.

It ought also here to be noted that the sorts of temptations are two, though their types are innumerable. The former kind are bitter and fearful; the latter are sweet and delightful.

All these temptations work together for good. They aggravate the true penitent's cry and longing for mercy, and they cause the children to stick closer to their heavenly calling, to promote humility, to wait upon God, and to experience that all blessings come from him alone.

The path of sanctification

When professing Christians, especially the young ones, come and tell us of their blessings under the Word, their comforts, and various feelings, we must not be too apt to heed them, nor encourage them too much to rely on such things, for that will neither be just in us, nor good for them; but rather exhort them to keep close to the Word and prayer.

Faith discovers what God has prepared for those that love him. Hope lays hold of it as faith discovers it. Faith is always diving deeper into the mysteries and mercies of God. It always goes a distance before our attainments. By this means we are always buoyed up in hope; that which we see in faith we shall enjoy. Thus we look in faith for the promises of God, for the grace yet further attainable in this life, and for the glory that shall be hereafter revealed in us. By these means also we are induced more closely to use and pursue the means of grace, yes and to press unwearily forward to the mark for the prize of the high calling.

In the morning at waking, as spiritual or temporal things get the first impression on the mind, they commonly prevail for the day. We therefore should be very watchful over our hearts, take care to begin as soon as we wake, with meditation, prayer or praise.

Self-examination and meditation

The more I look inward and search into the state of my own soul, or the more I speak with others about the spiritual state of their souls, the more I experience the ways of the Holy Spirit in and with the children of God.

Hence it is evident to me that we can never examine ourselves too much.

Self-examination and meditation are mighty helps in prayer. The former furnishes us with material, the latter with ardour and zeal. Therefore we should always use both before prayer, especially in the secret place. That barrenness and coldness in prayer that we so often feel and complain of is generally owing to the lack of this exercise.

Profiting from public worship

When any child of God by reason of extreme cold, snow or rain abstains from his class meeting or from public preaching, though he may and does take care to supply his absence by reading or other religious exercises at home, yet afterwards, they will have the worst of it. He will find more uneasiness by far in his conscience for his negligence on the aforesaid account, than all the distress or harm he could possibly have sustained from the inclemency of the weather.

We should never fail to search our hearts before we go to prayer: nor to pray before we hear the Word, if we expect either prayer or preaching to profit us.

One great way to a blessing is not to do, as many, it is feared, do, [to] rest upon men and means and so hinder the expected blessing; but to look through both at God alone. So shall you find your desires granted and your wants at all times supplied.

When we can engage in reading, hearing, meditating, singing or praying, let us always have those words of the Apostle in our minds: 'We are not our own, we are bought with a price, therefore let us glorify God in our body and in our spirit, which are God's' (cf. 1 Corinthians 6:19-20). This, as well as what we read, hear, meditate, sing or pray for, will mightily help to fasten our faith and our heart's affections and attention singly and reverently upon the Lord; by which wandering and distracting thoughts will be best kept away, and more sweet communion with God, and larger incomes of blessing, will be experienced by us.

The life of prayer

'Teach us to pray'

Praying Christians are growing Christians, for though they are not blessed for praying, yet I find, they are blessed in praying; and so may we say of every other means of grace, if we will speak as the truth is.

I am often troubled with wandering thoughts in prayer and more so when I join with others than when I pray by myself. And of all wandering thoughts the most deceitful are those which are apparently good and holy. Other sorts which arise from carnal objects that are suggested to the mind are more detestable. In prayer I have stopped sometimes when pious wandering thoughts perplexed me to weigh them up ... I had not prayed against them nor guarded against them as against the other [wandering thoughts], believing these to be less evil. But I have since found that neither these [pious thoughts] nor any other sort arise from my own mind except seldom. They come from Satan. I find that his design is to turn our thoughts from God; to break our communion with him and to cause us to displease him and to hinder our prayers entering his ears. And where at times other wandering thoughts are hated and resisted by us, Satan then for these wicked ends, puts on the form of an angel of light, and tempts us with pious wandering thoughts. Therefore we must reject them as well as other sorts of wandering thoughts, as great and pernicious obstructions to our addresses to God.

The same is the case when we are hearing the Word, either read or preached. Therefore let us diligently watch and pray to God to banish them from us.

Communion with God

We lose many a choice blessing, and much sweet communion with God through weakness of faith, negligence of prayer or indolence in it, and not keeping close to every other means of grace. For you will find more comfort from God when you are most diligent in using the means; and less comfort the less you use the means. So is it also with respect to the growth of grace.

Never did a soul go to heaven, I find, but his heart went there first. He first lives there in heart and affection, and then in person (Matthew 6:20; Colossians 3:1-2).

When I have for some time together enjoyed the light of God's countenance and to my own thinking have lived so long agreeably to his holy will, if I then give way to some temptation, or commit a fault, I am more apt to cover it or to vanish the appearance of it out of my thoughts, than to confess it. But I have no true ease in my heart until I have confessed it to God, and then I am delivered. O let me never cover, but immediately confess it. So shall I be at peace with him.

I have observed many people exceeding anxious while under convictions of sin for the blood of Christ as a sacrifice to wash and pardon them; but very indifferent and careless to have the Spirit of Jesus as a prophet and king to teach and govern. O this is a sore evil! A lively and flourishing Christian is as concerned through prayer and in communion with God to get a pure heart, free from all corruption (1 John 3:3) as a pardoned conscience free from all guilt and condemnation.

I find that the closer communion I have with the Lord and the more diligently I labour to walk in his ways, the more does the devil strive to beset me, and the more violent temptations assault me; and on the other hand, the more remiss, careless and heedless I am at any time, the less I am beset and assaulted.

When we have much of God's presence and great comfort, there shortly after follow grievous trials, and sore conflicts either from the world or from our own flesh [sinful nature]. Such comforts therefore are not only preludes, but preparatives for the evil day.

Meditation and prayer

I find reading and hearing the Word of God is good, but my experience is that private prayer, heart or self-examination, meditation and contemplation is far better. The former is necessary and justifiable; but the latter is as necessary and more profitable. The former is more human and increases head knowledge, while when conveyed from the head to the heart by the Holy Spirit, it will do us good; we shall also find that such Christians who read much but meditate, examine etc. little are generally, though wise and knowledgeable, barren, cold and lifeless; but the others are lively and fervent.

O how much sweet communion with God and how many weighty and soul-feeding, strengthening, comforting blessings do I clearly see Christians daily lose for lack of more exercise in this regard. O that I could for one hour's reading, meditate for five. How inconceivably further advanced should I be, were this but my case, in the grace of God, than at present I am, though with shame and grief I speak it. Dear souls, mind this.

I find I am slothful in prayer however conscious I may be of the need of it... Fervency, I am fairly satisfied, in prayer, though of no merit, yet is a necessary expedient to gain our petition. We must be wrestling Jacobs if we would be prevailing Israels.

Unanswered prayer

I have known myself and many others complain of praying a long time and could receive no answer to prayer and I have found these reasons amongst others for it.

a. Sometimes the lack of faith to receive that blessing desired. Therefore ... instead of plying God for the blessing, we should first pray for sufficient faith to receive it.

b. Sometimes the lack of stronger desires for the blessings. Faint desires produce but faint prayers — and God will never answer. Therefore such must get more fervent desires before their prayers will prevail.

c. Sometimes unthankfulness for past blessing will retard God's willingness to bestow the present ones. Beware of unthankfulness in this case.

d. Sometimes it is because the best seasons of God's giving and consequently of our receiving have not yet come. And therefore in such case we ought always to pray and not to faint. Were we always answered the instant we ask — such blessings would either prove curses, and some way or other bring grief to us, or they would lose their worth to us. Whereas, I find answers deferred, though a very long time, try our patience and affiance [trust], and when they come afford us good by being more precious. Moreover they make us more thankful and humble.

I find it often happens that I pray and I am never answered. And why so? Because the things asked for, I am persuaded at length, though not at first, God sees would do me more hurt than good. This I've often experienced to be the case and have found abundant cause to praise God for not answering me.

Providence and prayer

I have sometimes found myself at a stand to know whether my blessings were the effect of common providence or were answers to prayer. This is a thing that should be very closely examined, and which I believe we may clearly and satisfactorily resolve ourselves, in this way: If the blessings received (whatever they be) come from common providence (as do the blessings which the Lord bestows upon natural and unbelieving men) they will produce no thankfulness nor delight in God in the receivers. But blessings which are the answers to prayer fill the heart with more love for the Giver than for the gift itself; they excite the heart to praise God and motivate it to constancy in prayer afterwards.

And for the preacher

Times of deadness

When a preacher feels much lowness and deadness of soul before preaching, it forebodes great liberty to himself and much blessing to the people. This will teach him to be humble, to see his own insufficiency and weakness, and to look up to God alone for ability to speak, as the oracles of God, and for a blessing upon the hearers.

Times of encouragement

When a preacher has preached several times successively with great power and freedom, he is in great danger of sinking unconsciously into self-sufficiency or a selfish persuasion that he can go on in the same manner.

Whenever it is thus with him, he is sure to find himself in the next sermon he preaches, stripped of his power and liberty; or if he enjoy it, for ought he can perceive afterwards, it is void of blessing. Let us never forget to look wholly to God in profound humility for the whole success: and let us all remember, that though Paul may instrumentally plant, and Apollos water, God alone can give the increase.

Preaching Christ

Preaching Christ in all his offices, especially in his priestly one, is not only one of the best doctrines, but one of the best methods of exciting the love of God in our hearts and inuring us [or making us accustomed] to all holy conversation and godliness. So that the more we preach Christ — and that we can never do too much — the greater success shall our labours have, the more eminently blessed will the hearers be and the more will they abound in love and obedience to God. Indeed, when all exhortations to the most exact holiness of life shall fail, or, which is worse, have a tendency to making Christians of a legal spirit and at last to end in the flesh; I say and do affirm, that from preaching up the life, death, sufferings of Jesus Christ such love will arise, as is the best incentive, and strongest sanction in the world to a holy life. Therefore, by all means let us take care to preach up JESUS, and him crucified, or 'Christ is made unto us wisdom and righteousness and sanctification and redemption'. Whenever we decline from this method of preaching, the church will wane; but while we continue in it, the church will stand and flourish.

Nature and grace

I plainly perceive that the same grace, perhaps the same quantity of grace, works differently in different persons: nay, that little grace will do more in some persons than twice as much does in others. For in such as are naturally courteous, meek and mild a little grace will appear gracious; when in those of a sulky, sturdy, angry morose disposition by nature great grace, yea, very great grace will scarcely mollify them and set them out like the other.

How to discern a true believer

A child of God and a child of Satan, or, which is the same thing, a regenerate and an unregenerate person, are easily discerned. Whenever you meet with them, you may discover them in a quarter of an hour's discourse or less. Begin to discourse on a spiritual subject, to the one it will be agreeable and pleasant; to the other it will be disagreeable and irksome. The one will talk of nothing but the life and work of God in the soul of man but the other will talk of nothing but his trade, his farm or his yokes of oxen. Or if he talks of religion, all turns upon 'Do and Live'.

Encouragements and exhortations for all

Love all true believers

It is an invaluable benefit and unspeakable comfort to possess a spirit void of all bigotry and perfectly catholic. For I find by happy experience, that the nearer one attains through the grace of God our Saviour to such a spirit and frame of soul, the more do we enjoy of these two great blessings, among many more. First, his heart is cordially knit in love to every one of whatever opinion, persuasion, profession, or party of people he be, in whom he discerns and feels the Spirit, image, life and love and grace of the holy Jesus to be. And, secondly, he can draw benefit and comfort from *his* conversation equally as from [that of] those that are of the same persuasion, and profession with himself. And he has what may be called a third great blessing, a heart always at liberty to pray for the salvation of all mankind. But Oh! the lamentable mischief occasioned by party zeal, bigotry and partial opinion in the body of Christ's people, and in the breast of her private members. How carefully should we pray, how diligently should I and all professing Christians guard against it.

Study to talk less

Too much discourse and too many words about any temporal, though necessary, affair or thing, I find to be a great canker or barrier to God's grace in my heart. Therefore though I find myself naturally prone to it, yet I must either restrain it or suffer much loss in my soul.

Good out of evil

When I am, as it has often happened, in a lukewarm, lazy indolent frame of spirit, the Lord suffers me to fall into some heart-affection sin, to humble, quicken and rouse me up to diligence in my Christian vocation. Thus God, blessed for ever, blessed be his name, brings good out of evil.

Bear no grudges

I am fully persuaded that if I would be serviceable as God grant I may, to the souls of all, I must carry well to all; resent no injuries or affronts; pass by them, and like St Paul, so far as I can with good conscience, become all things to all men.

For the dying Christian

I think it ridiculous for a dying Christian to take leave of the church, since they are shortly to follow and all are to dwell together in glory with God. His dying words should be, 'I am going to heaven, to God, to glory a bit before you, while you are still getting ready, and as soon as ready, you will follow me.' If a man and his wife are invited to dine with a friend, and he sets out an hour before her, would he bid her farewell at his setting out, when both are to dine together at noon?

Christ precious

I feel that the more odious sin is, the more precious Jesus is to my soul and so vice versa.

Grimshaw's covenant and self-dedication to God

I do most solemnly and eternally give up, devote and dedicate myself, spirit, soul and body to my dear, and for ever blessed, Triune God. And to this solemn dedication and vow I do hereby solemnly invoke as witnesses thereto all the powers of heaven: God the Father, Son and Holy Ghost; all the holy angels and all the souls and spirits of just men made perfect. All the powers and solemn things on earth: the church, the Word of God, the Lord's Supper, men, earth, living creatures, sun, moon and stars. And if it matter anything, all that is in hell too, devils and all damned souls, to bear witness to this renewal of this my solemn dedication and vow to God.

Further reading

Frank Baker, *William Grimshaw 1708-63*, Epworth Press, 1963.

Faith Cook, *William Grimshaw of Haworth*, Banner of Truth Trust, 1997.

George C. Cragg, *Grimshaw of Haworth, A Study in Eighteenth Century Evangelicalism*, Canterbury Press, 1947.

Marcus L. Loane, *Cambridge and the Evangelical Succession*, Lutterworth Press, 1952.

John Newton, *Memoirs of the Late Rev. William Grimshaw, A.B. in Six Letters to the Rev. Mr Henry Foster*, Hamilton, 1814.

J. C. Ryle, *Christian Leaders of the 18th Century*, Banner of Truth Trust, 1978.

Three of Grimshaw's unpublished manuscripts have been used in this book. The fourth was made the subject of a paper by Paul Cook delivered at the 1995 Westminster Conference and entitled *William Grimshaw and the Admonition of a Sinner*. The conference report can be obtained from the Conference Secretary, Rev. John Harris, 8 Back Knowl Road, Mirfield, W. Yorkshire, WF14 9SA.

Other titles by Faith Cook...

Under the scaffold

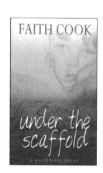

Imagine you are growing up in an eighteenth-century village high up in the Yorkshire Moors. Times are very hard, and you have to work long hours to help your family to have even the basic essentials. Disease and death are all around you — even the death of young children.

This is the life of Tom Whittaker. Early events left deep scars and many unanswered questions. Is there really a heaven? Does God hear prayer? How can I ever forgive?

Although Tom is a fictional character, his life of hardship was typical of the days in which he lived, and has been drawn from many true-life incidents. Most importantly, he comes into contact with William Grimshaw, the unconventional and fiery curate of Haworth. Grimshaw's desire to teach God's truth brought him into many a conflict, with even a riot against him and his friend John Wesley. Yet his love and care for his flock, and, above all, the message of hope and salvation he brought, changed the lives of thousands of men, women and children.

Under the scaffold, Faith Cook, Evangelical Press, 160 pages, ISBN-13 978-0-85234-597-9.

Fearless
pilgrim

John Bunyan is well known as the author of *The Pilgrim's Progress*, the seventeenth-century spiritual classic which has been the second best-selling book in the world after the Bible. He was also a much-loved preacher and pastor whom crowds flocked to hear after his release from prison. One contemporary wrote that he 'could weep for joy most part of his sermons'.

But how did Bunyan become such a preacher and writer? In this book you will discover the path which prepared him to be greatly used as a pastor to his own generation and a guide to Christ's pilgrim people still.

'In this new and well-written biography Faith Cook relates John Bunyan to the turbulent times through which he lived, surviving two periods of imprisonment in Bedford prison, sustained by his faith, determined, as he himself wrote, "to live upon God that is invisible"...'

David Kingdon

Fearless pilgrim, Faith Cook, Evangelical Press, 530 pages, ISBN-13 978-0-85234-680-8.

Lady Jane Grey
Nine-day queen
of England

Lady Jane Grey has often been called the 'Tudor Pawn' but to see her as one whose life was simply moved around by others is totally inadequate. In order to understand the full tragedy and triumph of her life it is vital to grasp the far-reaching political and religious changes that were shaking England at the time. The Reformation touched the whole population; from palace to university; from emerging town to peasant cottage.

Like a complicated jigsaw the pieces come together to give a picture of a girl with outstanding natural abilities, whose strength of character and remarkable faith shine out despite the darkness that often surrounded her. Executed at sixteen, Jane paid an awful price for a throne she did not seek.

Lady Jane Grey, nine-day queen of England, Faith Cook, Evangelical Press, 256 pages, ISBN-13 978-0-85234-613-6.

Our hymn-writers

and their hymns

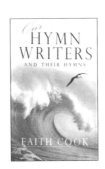

The people of God have always had cause to sing, and who has more reason to sing than the man or woman who knows the living God, the joy of sin forgiven and the certainty of a life to come? Throughout the Old and New Testaments, believers marked God's mighty acts of deliverance in song.

Hymns based on the great themes of the Christian message have their own unique ministry to mind and heart, renewing faith and hope in God especially in days of spiritual decline and apathy. In this work Faith Cook traces the development of the Christian hymn from the early period of the Christian Church to the present day.

Biographical sketches of a number of our best-known writers from the past figure here. We are also introduced to some of the lesser-known poets such as Paul Gerhardt, Samuel Crossman and Samuel Medley. Love for God and the great truths of the gospel shine out through the words of these men and women of faith. More than this, we also discover how their individual personalities and circumstances are reflected in the hymns they wrote.

Our hymn-writers and their hymns, Faith Cook, Evangelical Press, 400 pages, ISBN-13 978-0-85234-585-2.

Did you know that every time you buy one of our books you are helping someone else to do exactly the same? EP Mission www.epbooks.org

A wide range of Christian books is available from EP BOOKS. If you would like a free catalogue please write to us or contact us by e-mail. Alternatively, you can view the whole catalogue online at our web site:

www.epbooks.org

EP BOOKS
Faverdale North, Darlington, DL3 0PH, England

e-mail: sales@evangelicalpress.org

EP BOOKS INC.
P. O. Box 825, Webster, New York 14580, USA

e-mail: usa.sales@evangelicalpress.org